THE KING

THE KING

Poems

REBECCA WOLFF

W. W. NORTON & COMPANY

New York   London

For information about permission to reproduce selections from this book,
write to Permissions, W. W. Norton & Company, Inc.,
500 Fifth Avenue, New York, NY 10110

For information about special discounts for bulk purchases, please contact
W. W. Norton Special Sales at specialsales@wwnorton.com or 800-233-4830

Manufacturing by Courier Westford
Book design by Brooke Koven
Production manager: Julia Druskin

Library of Congress Cataloging-in-Publication Data

Wolff, Rebecca, 1967–
The king : poems / Rebecca Wolff. — 1st ed.
p. cm.
ISBN 978-0-393-06932-7
I. Title.
PS3623.O56K56 2009
811'.6—dc22

2009005781

W. W. Norton & Company, Inc.
500 Fifth Avenue, New York, N.Y. 10110
www.wwnorton.com

W. W. Norton & Company Ltd.
Castle House, 75/76 Wells Street, London W1T 3QT

1 2 3 4 5 6 7 8 9 0

For Asher

CONTENTS

THE LORD

DEPTH ESSAY

ACKNOWLEDGMENTS

My thanks to the editors of the following publications, in which these poems first appeared:

"The Letdown": 26

"Deeply Psychological"; "My Charge"; "Raised by Wolves"; "The Therapist": *The American Poetry Review*

"The Lord is Coming: All bets are off": *The Autumn House Anthology of American Poems and Prayers*, ed. Robert Strong

"In my Jesus year": *Awake!: A Reader for the Sleepless*, ed. Stephen Beeber

"Painting and Sculpture": *The Columbia Review*

"I am on drugs"; "You say there are no standards but there are": *Cross Cultural Poetics*

"The King": *Crossroads*, journal of the Poetry Society of America

"Laconic Parkway": *Fourteen Hills*

"I live in the rectory"; "I feel like letting my freak flag fly": *GutCult*

"Where's the Funeral?": *Jubilat*

"Content is King": *LIT*

"The Trick of My Life": *Women's Studies Quarterly*

"The King"; "You say there are no standards"; and "Breeder Sonnet": *Women Poets on Mentorship: Efforts and Affections*, ed. Arielle Greenberg and Rachel Zucker

"Attitudes at Altitudes"; "Nonfiction": *A Public Space*

THE KING

THE CONDITION

Tonal Pattern

Mothers to be on the floor
in a ring

A ring of mothers to be
                    unembarrassed

singing a progression.

But taking her own tail
                    up the ass

might interfere with the fetus.

I am on drugs

on an airplane

mentally

and there are some other things wrong with me

perennially
I have control over them

How's the soup today?
convivial
in the poor park

sipped from Styro
a gray rain drizzled in

My natural prey
(exactly what I wanted to say)

taking the airs

My natural airs
stop time while I move

I walk the junkie's walk (tilted)

yet somehow my unborn child
is protected

a degree of imperviousness
the wind and the rain
the hard shell
an impersonality

My natural predator
transgression: irresponsibility.

The child with all its natural immunity
will have been put on this earth

a test.

The Bawdy Mothers

A non-hybrid sexuality
(pure bred)

toes like nipples
in commune

implore you

their secret knowledge
not so secret

suppressed

Tower of Power
proportionally

Where did they ever get the idea
everything that comes out of my mouth

a kittenish

discussion of how long it is safe to labor
after the water breaks

Breeder Sonnet

corpulent
filament

rotting clams and oysters

I hate to wait
a liar and a thief
the underclass motif
posture of mean streets

a medium calm sweeps over the water
destroying the calm that was here before
a harbor—a tranquil, a desert of ocean
existed where nothing was here

it's kind of hard to say it with a
straight face: anxiety disorder
A special kind of "unhappy":

spiders and snakes

missed you.

Boo hoo.
Juvenate
and
rejuve
-nate

soot and suet together

a nice paste
for innovation

wake up wake up wake up

he said and slapped me

I deserved it/I was sleeping

in this defensive posture

Are you meant to be born
Were you meant?

a
b
a
b

c
d
c
d

e
f
e
f

g
g

Full Stop

Curling up a romance
twelve o'clock high. The day
creeping uphill away from
ecstasy. Week thirteen, three eggs *en plate*—
one of three things I did yesterday: Built
a humanoid, watched
it grow on TV where
"A Child is Born"
every day at some o'clock
when incandescence
roosts, crows,
the new poetry

a game for fools.
Back when I was born, my child, the poets
didn't know yet, just think,
they yet trod lightly,
they arose and went now to Innisfree.
They wrote this song for me.

Painting and Sculpture

There is a little dead one
out here on the deck,
a little live one
inside where we keep
all our lives. Lives inside,
so far as we are able,

and outside big trees, shaking
all night in the wind,
shelter creatures
we cannot contain
or imagine
or bear up under
or misprize.

Inside, at night, the horse-face
looms, large as a monument,
while a small monument
makes shapes
on the table.
It is day. Outside, flat

in the light,
holds a candle.
I in my area
have not arrived at
shapes, seen so clearly when they are
abstracted.

That is the hope
of the creature inside me,
that is the species
whose will be done, that will be the work of the captive
portion.

Creative Visualization

In real time
cells divide

A capital soup
Army of waiting

mixed with
expectancy

expansion ruled by
contraction

Yoga mat
suggests

Golden heat
golden light
golden rays
everything higher than I can get
golden for the meantime

Until the real color
comes

Poem on Colostrum

Coming down early,
a favorable sign
unhindered
this rendition
like a hook
and it caught

there is always
the case
no other case
this case
package

together and all in order
taking advantage of every good fortune
packed

in favor
the habit of making
good body
moves to make
make the move

make the milk.

Third Poem of the Day: Insanity

I'm pregnant, you see
and it takes a lot out of me
and puts a lot in—three
has some ecclesiastical trinity
to it, and I provide, for free,
the third. Don't you think that it be-
trays an underlying vulnerability?
So far it pays no fee,
it rides for free. And takes, honestly,
its toll, in the form of psychic energy.
That amorphous palliative. So until the
proud September day when we see
a face, a shoulder, a wee
rump emerge, bloody, unscathed, we
hope, I cannot promise any
further payment of the penance due to thee.

Deeply Psychological

Heavy with child
up at dawn
I listen and listen to the racket of the birds
but they do not wait for a response
before they ask another question.

So many things seem at an end.
What doesn't is obvious
and bears no contemplation
or song.

And then I surfaced
a whole matrix
or rubric

magical thinking
other kinds of thinking
but in layers, you understand,

with supremacy
a honeycomb.

THE BABY

Laconic Parkway

I had a baby

it was inevitable—
I was pregnant

I live in the rectory

I detest intimacy.
I did not think, I only acted.
I married the pastor.
I dream about the feelings,
meditate on straw.

I don't imagine you've ever felt this way
(one of several ways)
(an ecstasy)
yet I can't tell the difference
between myself (momentarily)
and that one over there
and this is another syndrome

You can't remember how good it feels
What can you remember how good it feels?
I dare you to [ ]
(love, being in love, sex in love, transcendental massage)

I gave birth on my hands and knees
that is what I wanted to tell you

Remember you are the Goddess
in the room

You say there are no standards but there are

behaviors

sticks, rods
entreaties what cause shame

Varieties of morning.
I trade in that

Dawn—a more retractive
a "less and less"
—am revising.

Most of all to be at my leisure
is most important to me

As a witch I have to be conscientious
the energy I expend
contradiction next to me
a mutual breast

contradiction accepts me
a necessary levy
eroded standards
next to me a mutual breast
Font Royale
we mindlessly rifle
your pages
while we nurse

About breast milk

there is nothing
to say—it wraps you in layers

You wrap it in layers.
What's the lowest thing

that you understand?

It runs in his veins.

Royally
my heart was heavy with it

my hands tingle with the urge
to receive him

Nothing will ever stay the same again
and that is what I asked for

His body in
my body

breaks you open

Excitation of the Banal

Peer anxiously into his face:
bathe his sleeping head in shadow
The sound of the wind in the trees—banal

my reward
In Connecticut

I see the moon, stars, suns, planets
as if for the first time from the front seat
of a wrecker.

I take my hand away but I
leave my energy

under his eyes purple shadows
mountain range reflected in a shallow
pool

A little piece of fluff
on the side

In my arsenal I have one breast
the shadow of my one remaining hand, patting

There's something ineffable I do
to make the baby grow
a day older

A Page from Cathy's Book

Resume treatment
when treatment is due

Two tasks at once
not multi but at least

pumping while clenching
optimism, a chain of

conception then visitation
visitation and conception

and it's kind of like this:
I don't care if you think I'm crazy

I am crazy

but our sons will be brothers

The sun is what we see by

A pale light shines in on us
this morning

What he loves me for
I do in secret

It will always come back—
not so brilliant after all

Your devotions

elicit a letdown
love the letdown

A little piece of fluff
on the side

of your head
a little bit of fluff
on the side of the road

dead incidentally
the inarticulation kills me

frees my right hand up to do
what my left hand cannot bear

Where's the Funeral?

In anticipation of the body
a quartet of horsemen stand

at a safe distance from the shore

the corporeal a baby
I bodied forth.

(And I am watching at the shoreline
collecting seashells
while I ingest

something special
to induce forgetfulness.)

Fruits are related,
but this here is a made thing:
No horses, no dividend:
the rideless nucleus.

In black, all in black,
as though to mock
a mother's sorrow.

You cannot have the body

until you make me one
in exchange.

The Letdown

I think that I shall never see
A poem lovely as a tree.

A tree whose hungry mouth is prest
Against the earth's sweet flowing breast

—*"Trees,"* JOYCE KILMER

The little boy
with the scales

stepping-stone
wishing well
harbinger

(keeping it)
close to the breast

You have suffered a great disappointment

•

The story of milk
its manual expression

hard enough to remember
one's lessons
day to day

All things being what they are,
here it is.

where there's milk
there's (life) (hope)
something to eat in the emergency

•

and
writhing

I wiped that smile
right off your face

and by withholding
the milk from my breast

make a man out of you

[and with [my raving

I wouldn't wish this
on anyone

not even a mother

•

Rarely has "the death
instinct"

been so patiently expressed

Through no fault of my own

I reabsorbed the milk
I had made

but I could not reabsorb
the one whom I had made

to feed.

•

I dreamed I nursed my baby

at my breast. In a rocker

on a steamship

by a porthole

the horizon.

What a crazy dream.

I came by it honestly

lost it brutally

word in mouth.

•

The only subject upon which I have any authority
woke me from my sleep

The breast an ambassador

he only remembers it, shockingly
as long as he needs to. His head turns
in for the sweet

nothing and then I weep.

Can we talk reasonably about the fact
that everything's going to be
all right?

A scheme, that's what it is

to put the hammer through
a sieve,

because now everything means something

The groaning board
where I lay him out

•

It made a big impression on her,
her friend weeping copiously, unchecked,
over the newborn.

"Under the sun
we nearly died of
worry. My response
to worry is weeping. A lifetime
of worry: Pale petal pink, or
the color of eggshells."

•

The V of her gown had been pulled aside

but you can't nurse on a dead mother

•

soy milk
heavy cream
organic whole
simulated
it's like I lost the baby
it's not like I lost the baby
at the beginning I wished
sometimes I'd lost the baby

•

the living baby
grew
growing backwards upstairs
into the abstract

a rosy-faced
anybody

I can't do anything
with him

take the sky, and everything else
Let's look at the sky and everything else
a strange tale, if anyone will tell it

no compromise,
some of the most inspired, yes,
everything in quotation marks

and the milk spurts
Lurid,
peaceful Christmas

THE KING

Nonfiction

I make my pancakes from scratch,
mind you

but the decorative arts in general
leave me cold

Consequently I know
very little of the world.

That's the way they greet me—
that's the way they have always

greeted me:
a fire in the eyes

and dedication
to the experience
in the moment.

Self-Interest

the babe, the carriage
what is best?
the rainy street
my occlusion of it
insistence upon
my dominion over it

the sheltered
occupation of it
my greatness o'ershadowing
perambulation
distinct meters
unlocked steppes

statisticians dominate
the field of inquiry
—paralyzed with fear
as per the chart of probability
and with your actions and neurotic
repetitions you perpetuate their accuracy

one's sweater in daylight:
it is dotted with food,
embroidered with long, brown hairs

only to be upbraided next
by the mother-in-law

who moves instinctively
to shield her son.

Handlers protect me
from myself

Content is King

I queen it

over emptiness.

I invent it, a surplus,
a bombast of nervous

encryption so the process
of blanking becomes

isometric—Pilates.
I think of how clueless

and relentless-
ly depthless

my mother, nonetheless
she birthed and hers

is the aspect
and prospect

the matter
and subject

and

gangway.
I find something to say.

The king is content.

The Continuing Adventures

Graveside
We don't need no
decorative objects

My bridge and my
ticket to the bridge

separated at birth
a perfect plot: What
would the Puritans do?

Grow up and form attachments
Form heterosexual attachments,
or homosocial,

or symbolic, to tall
buildings.

Go down to see the wreckage.
What does it inspire but
vengeful thoughts

as a blow job looks like
submission
to the casual observer

a dream of bad breath
Convenience slut/whore to convenience
Little teeth where you might sit

and actually physically
see the avenue
engendering proximity.

How green was my valley

its crop circles and
burial mounds

conjoined hallucinations
Graveside
"riverine"

opportunistic and demeaning

at the same time: How can that be?

The paper is there, the pen is there,
on my back the saddle
or other accommodations

A sun dress:
Have you never had the experience
(a complete reversal
saw the other side in its entirety
it swallowed).

King I

Alone at last with my feelings,
the King an unlikely sentry

the king a peculiar
the king a makeshift

Thinking is dry, and frivolous

I often have a hidden agenda
                    (a secret)

King II

And why the King should choose
to starve his son to death,
in isolation
and torture him with
water running pitiless on his nakedness,

I'll never know.

I woke up, changed.
You've got to spend money
to make money.

King III

In the kingdom
you will live together forever
because she is a fag
hag and you are a fag
hag hag. Family

foundation.

King IV

I wanted to make my son
look like a king

but I could not bring myself
to bind his forehead
to flatten the back of his head
on a flattening board

Generally I am opposed to mutilation

Even manipulation

THE MAN

Taking a Walk with You

Windy morning
when there is nothing wrong with me
faint smile
faint agitation

I have a message (for the dead)
to deposit
at the graveyard

Very quiet
the very quiet stories
a wet morning
and they don't give you
any place to sit
kicking around

the graveyard
as an origin
it's more of a destination

shapes in nature
(rest in peace)

there's no call for making something.
Walking uphill this is your mind

it is not enough anymore to be a figure
in a landscape

Unless Balthus
a portal to anonymity
I can't tell you the name
because it is of no
self-importance.

It dawns on me
that you would always
rather
be alone.

Trade

And then of course there's the whole question of retaliation.

—DAN RATHER

A kind of glee
and its surviving twin

The rickety footbridge
A boost to the economy

the brighter side
Lie down with the lighter

dead
Coincidentally noon bells indicate

from now on there is no such thing
as an irrational fear

the path of early fall sung along by dying
crickets, littered with dead

crickets in the path to the cocoon
of early fall

Bombs,
Triggered by invention

Devastation by decorum
invented before cars

in the cocoon we build our salt-box mansion
inside the saltbox there are many mansions

Just a few steps away a rotting hulk
harboring extraterrestrial life

Our first kiss of the morning
salty, in exchange

commemorates the true day,
not the day on which it occurred

You say you always liked the way there were two of them,
and they were whatever color the sky was.

"And what to do with the rest of the day?"—Dan Rather
and its surviving twin.

A little human contact?
The poem must end.

The Lees

Song of faithful love
song of infidelity

eyes downcast in modesty . . . Lowell . . . Hardwick—
how those people did get married!

Cradle—a noun entirely outmoded
but a verb in use today

Because you do change (McCarthy . . . Rahv)
because the person

makes you into another person (McCarthy . . . Wilson).
This is why it makes a difference

. . . to say it
much less think it!

I love two men
or maybe three

away from home: only soft clothing
against my soft skin

on the road trip
away from home

I am not sleeping
only resting

the way back
is a tree house

he would give me even
his name

Investiture of Human Voice

The scroll that flags
on the vine—I found
it again and fly it
now for the benefit of
what could be mine.

What could be yours: discreet
caricature of the loving heart
the suffering the Buddhist
finds your knees pressed against
the back of the fat man's
groaning seat. I mean to say

something here! Not to enact
or reference—the dead
itself, stove in for the benefit,
the conscripted heart
of the human voice, a better
means of keeping the rote
at bay. Intractable command,
the errant lyric all at sea,
another contested humanity.
Is it so cruel to tell a story?

I started out with a different end.
The things that make a grown man
happy in front of my very eyes—

I watch you read.

The Trick of My Life

How like sound, to be a song.
Why are you doing that? Are you doing it because you
    want to?
Here he comes,
I am on the table. Everyone is listening.

Liniment on treasured eyelids
I am so much better now at saying what I want

scented oil in a circular motion
and sutured orifice
rictus the mask.
The balm he addresses to me

and a wild responsive snatch
make the choice between
abandon and commitment to memory
easy.

As he will write it down for me
Siren of modulation

bring a cup and tissue where I lie

shrouded in simultaneity.
Are you all right? I am all right

I could not call a halt now if I tried.
endless curiosity
wheelchair of curiosity

From now on I never will say what I want
or tell him when it hurts
I will make him do what he wants to see what happens when
   he does.

Everyone is on the table
used and attended
I am listening
I would not call a halt now if I could.

I paid for it
or it was given to me as a gift
not incoherent.

They say a stench of blossom burst from the corpus when my
   spine burst
with the thrust

abandoned at the last.

Namely

There's a feeling I get—
sap rising in the renegade column
colossal anti-destination—
it's a think-about/not-think-about.

The curtailed
fell on me.
Poem of longing, *achtung*,
doctor's-office style. Your light
under a bushel, emotional register. You have robbed me of my
nameless potential: I recognize in myself and represent
that coveted worker
who never falls ill. Stole

my audience. One
who will not be conjured.
If it does not return to you
that's the idea: sitting duck/moving target. Others
crowd out, leaving a poison: *Thou.*
Ravishment effected: All strung along on

achievement: to slit myself open lengthwise
for you, or, failing that, to
spread my legs wider than is humanly possible—
doctor's-office style. This feeling I've got:

from where I stand I can see
the Rose Café—
the street goes one way
and it goes another. Juncture

condition: You reflect or deflect the maundering seascape,
you engage the hummingbird's
cryogenic adventure, you encourage me to
make a choice: The big spoon will not fit
comfortably in my mouth, but the smaller spoon . . .
    Addressee.
Who I can leave,
when the day is done.

Different People Feel Differently

Everything makes a little noise
                              (sense)

Suddenly, there was a ball in the box

More purposeful now than before

the ninth of ten boxes

it rolls because it's rounded
it doesn't have any corners

concentric—but not circular.

A really decisive move: He found
my poems in a box

before I was dead.

Here is a feather.

It's how birds
move around. (One
in a million—part
of many parts.)

He feels just the same as I do,
about everything.

THE BABY

I feel like letting my freak flag fly

It's never the end . . .

1967 all over again

I had a tail
was a stubborn

commingler—insisted
on being held.

Now round and round
again my fat head

rests
some soft stuff all around my head

The consolation of poetry
the smell of my head a consolation

instead of talking to myself

Now I talk to Him
Hard won
Firstborn

Careworn
Drained, literally.

Erotics (Normative)

You remind me of what is normative

the miracle of flight
the flight of human thought
growth of the vitamin industry—
nutrients, outside the body!—
price-fixing; that it can be done.

GMOs—undercarriage made in hell—
the illusion of perspective
exquisite chinoiserie!
flight in air eating fish.

Monstrous custodian
of the left hand,
conspicuously self-absorbed

You—
one with the universe—
refresh my memory

His Winning Ways

The luck of the ages.

When he's not cheerful he's

meditative

I'm tempted
to turn and look at him

and so I do.

Often I whisper

a source of great anxiety

Often I speak to him reasonably
"The caterpillar must become a butterfly
                              eventually"

Out of pressure arises concentration
out of concentration a kind of fission

Could you say Elephant?
Could you say Tiger lily?

Acquisition
a solitary confinement

intercom:

between house
and guesthouse

He has his knees around his ears like
(contingency)
a little porn star

You kiss his feet

You must look into his eyes
as though you really knew him
(and not shy away)

You must kiss him behind the knees
(where you have never kissed another)

My Charge

That child has the luck of the ages.

All the luck.
It strains atheism

but not to the breaking point. A new breed,
hands, feet, taste buds,

solar panel
extra-sensitive, responsive to

any change.
It's no accident

all the congenital stuff
works fine

(like a charm),
the rhetoric of

"God's glory filling you"
what escapes my body

through a tiny slit in the palm of my hand.

The baby idealized his mother

while she was away.

When she returned he found it
difficult to integrate
his vision
with the reality:
strong arm,
overbite, protective
coating.

The Erotics of the Baby

The feeling is mutual

(from) one container
to another

Just because I am tender
does not mean I am a mother

cry for no reason
drink the same water
that he drinks

the sound the wind makes in the trees
for him

all minor dramas

Why here? For there is more opportunity
to do good here

Lost in thought, the baby

Primarily

I am a mother.
When he was sick;

I engaged his imagination
with a book—

the perfect—I seized it; his
weakened defenses.

This is the way I have
filled his mind

egg and milk and butter and bread
all together—

that's a lot for a small child to take in.
Like Maisie

in the novel is a sieve.
What we want to cultivate in him:

A fat man's
personality on a thin man.

The Good-Enough Mother

rolling ball of thunder

discomfited by
change of venue

It's better to have a feeling
than a thought—

I got overheard
I got overexcited

Snow fell on the ground
making the heavens warmer.

He sneezed twice,
and lay on the ground also,

lazily sketching an angel's
wings with his wings.

Daddy Long-Legs (One-Year Birthday)

He will be big in August.
He sleeps in the dark,

where we cannot see him.
Will he ever be at rest,

ever again?

A *sh- sh- sh-* and a
short sharp shot

the arrow-leafed aster.
The orange moth, with pale

pink wings, with one
white eye on either wing,
parked for days on the screen
will shed his skins to become
a more beautiful moth—
where we can't see it.

"Stop eating me, Mommy
Stop eating me"

To everything, indeed:
purple coneflower
Daddy Long-Legs

the growth cannot be contained.

Today he tasted blood,
perhaps for the first time.

His own blood.
In his own mouth.

Raised by Wolves

I was so afraid he might run into
the road

I berated him senselessly.
For he is not even
two years old

on a cul-de-sac.
Our house lies somewhere at the end of a road.

At one end, a graveyard; at the other, a recreational playing
    field. At another end,
another graveyard. Our house lies at the end of a road.

Fox cub on the road
a demonstration of glass breaking
in order:

I was thinking about the road

and then he walked up behind me and said "have you dropped
    it yet?"

I have always sat in the road. Something says "Boo,"
and I run all the way down the road without looking behind
    me. In the dark
the moon is bright but doesn't help.

I don't remember the presence of another on the road, but it
    is difficult to imagine that I
would have been allowed to go alone.

Today I dragged him screaming down the road, by the wrist.
He wanted to go the other way.

THE LORD

Because He So Loved

Short eyes

moral compass

You're wasting your finest thought

on me

peaceable kingdom.

Everyone who is a god—

come before me:

suckling, toes, gesture, magisterial handling
of snake and sceptre, sister
of mercy just don't make
me eviscerate myself
I rely too much on the irony
that comes from inside.

•

The time I

broke my silence

was the last time in the hold
no stimuli

I left the room
I ate a handful of calcium
and blacked out in television

•

"These words I say to you"
that was the full extent.

Such an organized religion:
If I can't have sense
and I can't have nonsense

and the onus is on me to grapple
thrice over

and the vocabulary has left me and come upon me
at the same time
just as I always prayed when I cursed myself

•

Gehazi is snow-white with leprosy.
Is it funny for you to know
you are the only one who comes inside me?

A more significant, lasting King of Kings,

I'll let you do the talking for me
You know what it's like inside me.

In my Jesus year

Long story short
I got no sleep
sprawled out like a cat:

You start doing it
and then you learn you are in
the grand tradition

gloom is terrifying
comes with its own font
a dose of cremation

in the chamber
set on constant agitation
You see me not only at my worst

but in the grips
of an exalted digression
Rainspot

rainspot
the streets will be rinsed
clean in the morning but I dare

not visit.
With only my body to express
intention

My mind to confer
character

and the threat or treat of sunspot.
Put my cap on:
I escape that bad night

and set my cap for—
put a cap on . . .

Holy terror
all my life I had asked for
an inarguable

treatment
like Alice James did
white sheet

in the black
carapace.
Who are you that stands around and shakes

who are you that rolls the waves
who are you that steals cool from the air
and makes this morning for me.

Reduced Circumstance

The unfolding of the spirit occurs in the pathos of saying
  "God is good" when one knows
in fact that he is NOT—

the depiction of this in film and book
rat-strewn hovels, withering children,
wailing Mahalia Jackson—

and suddenly I'm given to feel awfully morally superior,
aren't I?

For a straphanger.

Scourge makes sense. If I had an ark I might fill it and
  dispense
with all the rest. God, in the down times, had a bright idea
  about everything on earth

perishing. Not an arbitrary judgment: a final solution.
Joseph practiced divination:
If you don't know the grandeur of that story then you are one
  of millions.

I believe my wisest course of action
would be to behave, immediately, as though it were the
  nineteenth century.

And come back in, eyes brilliant
from the whipping.

The Lord is Coming: All bets are off

I want to marry a toy maker
outside of my community
get so-and-so to interrupt
the motivational speaker

his eyes appear to be gray.
Hovels and shacks
in the huddle of city limits
within the constraints of my boundaries

Soon I shall be released

to the previous.

In the shadow of the street
the handsome recognize
the handsome. His eyes in the immediacy
appear to be gray. Now live together forever.

Why does it have to be so previously . . . ?

Extremely clever, to make it that way,
the urge for the love of God all in the past,
loving god or man all out of proportion

to his creation: windup toy,
stuffed dimension. To the question,

your only possible answer:
She's *natural*

The sweater is *deep black*
The sleeves are *casually pushed up*
naturalistic

Sound of wild animal
running from spider
the tall grasses
immaculate sound

glass animals of God
hauled before the tribunal
nailed into position
freed from the freedom

in the service of which I have been.
Have you been seen by me? In the
shadow of the shadow
          and disappeared

into composition:
in the shade of greater longing,
what little do I want from an encounter anymore?

Set piece, a constitutional

trot in vernal time
the cankerous fear of his coming
unrealized: "People are talking about . . ."

mechanical accompaniment
precipitous mountains

the accompanying
spirits rising up
through deep infernal forest
fog-drenched but not beset

exactly: reluctant to countenance the import
fresh slick on my lips
when I go to meet you

Why do you have to be so previous?

your eyes appear to be gray
outside of your environment.
The god in you greets the god

in me summarily and we proceed:
experiment in shared reality.

Lord how I wept when I came upon it (you)
I forget when last I had it (you).
I must be in the middle now, the dead
middle. On either side, morass.
Veiled valley. Audiovisual
one word now. Hand out
for greeting, demand made upon me
I register as erotic. Experiment

in shared reality: We gather together
to ask the Lord questions.

Moments before his arrival
I was alerted to his presence
Mother let me sit and stand
stand for a moment
while I regain perspective

I went down the staircase and there was no reentry.
If I fell in love with you

hand out
on the open market

a toy offering in the shadow of
the receding backside of Yahweh

Go with me

and be absorbed.

DEPTH ESSAY

Attitudes at Altitudes

The other side of the mountain
collects
and even cultivates
its mystery

I'm quite secular myself
but I have no problem
with religion

in fact I encourage it

How do I encourage it?

You might ask.

With my sentences. . . .

Vantage point . . .
Plate-blue sky . . .
Plateau of clouds . . .

Good God.

They trail off.

For the Shared Purpose of Music

Wanting to feel
and feeling so
(are) (are not)
one and the same

wanting to feel . . .
                    cozy . . .
        . . . Scottish

and the things about other people
that are beyond your control:

their catastrophic depressions, etc.

I like to harvest

it promotes

regrowth—
harmonious contact with the mothership

"the burden of possessions"—this, the kind
of monolithic idea

if you like that sort of thing

wild growth

as long as the babe sleeps
unattended
in the open house

shot through with air

it is the best way to sleep

Dry Western Spring

All the wildlife at eye level

scrambling for fallen fruit

old lady portaging knee deep over a

field of blown

dandelions

Here's what I see and

that's what I think.
Wild arugula, perhaps, growing free-range,
stinky

free-ranging, stinkily

in the tall desert grasses

in the unaccustomed wet,

for all I know,
or care to know.

What do I care to know about it?

Back-Formation

Because I'm so smart
I don't have to think about it

I just want it

and it is mine

as in infancy—
chug-a-lug

Therefore I mean nothing.

When I say it

I mean nothing by it

I don't know you when you

read it.

Gored by intent.

Bored by content.

That's why I love

transvestites—

or perhaps I am bored

by transvestites

their thin disguises.

There Are Certain Relationships That I Don't Understand

to this house
(I own it)

to this boy
(I made him, his whole body)

What is my relationship to the man's sleeping head
I don't know him

And the mother
(regarded, regretted, enabled, held the door)

A History of Depression

Find a shallow stand of pines
a shallow pun
or some other off, odd, verging place
the knot at the end of a line.
(Sit there and recall.)
When it ceases to throb and glow

cease taking orders: You command,
in your grasp, a unicorn,
or some other damned, faux-virginal
beast: Paleface on the gospel path,
damp.
Inclined to list.

The Therapist

I took her inside

myself

consumed

absorbed

less work

than carrying a hot child

four blocks

everything she said

was what I said

to myself

less work

than a friend

I suggest

you use her too

my friend

my child

[fell asleep beneath the magnolia]

went to sleep one place

[but woke up in the warm house]

woke up another.

There's a house for sale

on the corner. It takes
effort to understand

inside, inside
and every day.

Could I be inside the house

forever.

Charnel House

That night I fell asleep before
I could take my medication.

A ruined nest, dropped and blackened
past distinction by fire

and sodden in the rain, infant inhabitants
now one inhabitant. Gazed in sorrow.

Why I would dream that I do not know.
Everything's fine

Anxiety Rivals

invention

a lodestone

the gemlike

arrivistes

my children

revolving

dismantle anxiety apparatus

with

positive resource installation

Deep Down

attended to

over matter

The Breeze

has invented
alternative

to hermetic.

Elvis
laughed
blew

through the building.

Old Boyfriends

Now I am going to attempt to recapture the feeling of
  promise I had in my youth.
On breezes, long lines.
Essay on meditation. A reverie: that's what I mean—the
  whole situation of reverie, and
the smells accompanying the sounds of songs.

Something about Elvis that makes me cry (capable of deep
  feeling despite)
According to Gillian Welch he
"put on a shirt his mother made"—perhaps I am more a
  mother
than what other

Set myself up for the summer with the perfect
deck shoes—should make it possible
to feel deeply

For a short time I could

see beneath
the first layer. The man

hugged the tree
with one arm
and wielded
the chainsaw
expertly
with the other.

When you swim

you have to move

your arms and

kick your legs.

When you float,

you don't move at all—
lie very still on
the water.

He loves me best when
I teach him things.

He sounds like the teakettle,

crying.

Water, so miraculous; degrees of

miracle?

The history of water:
what is it,

in a book at my fingertips

at my disposal.

It

You have to find a good

recipe, one that's not too

sticky, or brittle,

or calcified.

I guess I never thought too much

about baking cookies.

Well think about it.

Isn't it interesting how,

on a rainy day,
when the boy is sick,
if you put your mind to it,
and then you take them out of the oven

—it's like magic!

To explain. Hard.
Like a friendship.
And now I know you better!
And I made a metaphor.

Thank you for my delicious breakfast

A wind picks up abruptly
while I am outside waiting
for my hot food. I do wonder,
politely, about its origins:
"Where did it come from?"

My lips tilt,
under the umbrella, slashed
with a cold rain—*lips* a word
like *mind*; no one ever
believes I am from New York City.

But it is true.
But my mother is from Tennessee.

What was it I liked about childhood?

The familial release of odors
upon a woodland walk at dusk. Flowering shrubs
play a not insignificant part. Elaborately formal, their
    mention.

I wandered lonely as a cloud
and never knew that poem until now—
reentered the house dim with umlauts, to find
the floor cool as milk under my feet.

And sought my mother's usual greeting,
wordless; father's approval,
insupportable; and knew it all as all there was:

Tartare, salted on the butcher's white waxed paper; avocado
eaten from its shell; statutes one can never learn too well.

We've had our children

now what do we do
with them?

I see you leading them
by the hand
a stumbling line
on a walk
down the

block to

deconstruction.
All the live long day.
Infants knock

their heads
against
an unyielding shoulder
in search of milk.
Metaphorical shoulder. Real

milk. A category
of relation
called I Hunger. I've had

my children and cannot
take that back. Buddhists call

it suffering.

Sotto Voce

I have never been a "thinker"
but still I require time alone
with my thoughts

Listening at the elbow of the great poet
I can feel a heart beating

inside me
a faster heart.

Oh!
I do not have to be a teacher
I can be the student

but never will I return to school.
No, not in this rainmaker costume.

Fat cells

and the cache
all my wisdom
all tendresse

to release it is attrition

for example
why may I not use thank-you
for my grateful
wretched
soul?

Why may I not use soul,
and the full sentence?

And the contrivance
of smile,
and simile.
My young son, in white
on the bearskin,
my new daughter, upstairs,
asleep on the lamb's.